NATIONAL GEOGRAPHIC

T0302853

THE LAND AROU

Plains

MARY TULL

PICTURE CREDITS
Cover, pages 9 (border), 11 (left and border), 13 (border), 15 (border), 17 (border), 19 (border), 21 (border), 23 (border), 25 (border), 27 (border), 29 (border), 30–31 (background) Terry W. Eggers/Corbis; page 1 Steve Bloom; pages 2–3, 23 Royalty-Free/Corbis; pages 4–5 (background) Felicia Martinez / Photo Edit; page 4 Ariel Skelley/Corbis; pages 6–7 (background) Barbra Leigh/Corbis; page 8 Tom Bean/Corbis; pages 9 (left), 31 (bottom) Jeff Vanuga/Corbis; pages 9 (bottom), 21 Darrell Gulin/Corbis; page 10 Setboun Michel/Corbis Sygma; page 11 (top right) Jason Edwards/National Geographic Image Collection; page 11 (bottom right) Dean Conger/Corbis; page 12 Stone/Getty Images; page 13 (left) Owaki-Kulla/Corbis; page 13 (right) Peter Beck/Corbis; page 14 Jay Dickman/Corbis; page 15 Corbis; page 16 Yann Arthus-Bertrand/Corbis; page 18 O. Louis Mazzatenta/National Geographic Image Collection; page 20 Richard T. Nowitz/Corbis; page 21 (top left) Raymond Gehman/National Geographic Image Collection; pages 21 (middle left), 25 (top) W. Perry Conway/Corbis; page 21 (bottom left) Tom Murphy/National Geographic Image Collection; page 22 Beverly Joubert/National Geographic Image Collection; page 24 Index Stock Photography; page 25 (bottom) T.H. Benton and R.P. Benton Testamentary Trusts/Licensed by VAGA, New York, NY. "Threshing Wheat" by T.H. Benton, in the collection of the Swope Art Museum, Terre Haute, IN; page 26 Layne Kennedy/Corbis; page 27 Larry Lee Photography/Corbis; pages 28, 29 Fermilab Visual Media Services; page 31 (top) Richard Hamilton Smith/Corbis; page 32 Michael Nichols/National Geographic Image Collection.

Produced through the worldwide resources of the National Geographic Society, John M. Fahey, Jr., President and Chief Executive Officer; Gilbert M. Grosvenor, Chairman of the Board; Nina D. Hoffman, Executive Vice President and President, Books and Education Publishing Group.

PREPARED BY NATIONAL GEOGRAPHIC SCHOOL PUBLISHING
Ericka Markman, Senior Vice President and President, Children's Books and Education Publishing Group; Steve Mico, Vice President, Editorial Director; Marianne Hiland, Executive Editor; Anita Schwartz, Project Editor; Jim Hiscott, Design Manager; Kristin Hanneman, Illustrations Manager; Diana Bourdrez, Picture Editor; Matt Wascavage, Manager of Publishing Services; Sean Philpotts, Production Manager.

ART DIRECTION
Dan Banks, Project Design Company

BOOK DEVELOPMENT
Nieman Inc.

CONSULTANTS/REVIEWERS
James F. Marran, Social Studies Chair, Emeritus, New Trier Township High School, Winnetka, Illinois
Dr. Margit E. McGuire, School of Education, Seattle University, Seattle, Washington

BOOK DESIGN
Steven Curtis Design, Inc.

MAP DEVELOPMENT AND PRODUCTION
Dave Stevenson

DIAGRAM DEVELOPMENT AND PRODUCTION
Steven Wagner

Published by the National Geographic Society
Washington, D.C. 20036-4688

Product No. 4J41758

ISBN-13: 978-0-7922-4564-3
ISBN-10: 0-7922-4564-4

Printed in the U.S.A.

21 20 19 18 17 16
11 10 9 8 7 6 5 4

Page 1: Masai herders in Kenya

Table of Contents

What Is a Plain? 4

Where Are the World's Plains? 6

Climate Makes Grasslands 9

Grasslands Have Different Names 11

People Farm on Plains 13

Grasslands Protect Soil 15

Herders Live on Plains 17

Ranchers Need Grasslands 19

Plains Provide Habitats 21

Plains Are Natural Wealth 23

Plains Are Beautiful 25

Grasslands Are a Disappearing Resource 27

People Bring Grasslands Back 29

Visual Literacy 30

Glossary 32

What Is a Plain?

A large area of flat land is a **plain**. Most plains are covered with grass. In areas where little rain falls, plains grasses are short. Where there is more rainfall, the grass on a plain can grow very tall. Plains grasses have deep roots that hold the **topsoil**. Topsoil is the layer of soil on the surface of the ground.

Plains do not have many trees. Where there is more rain, there will be more trees. Where there is little rain, plains will have few or no trees.

Grasslands in warm regions are homes to many different kinds of animals. Colder grasslands have far fewer kinds of animals.

Human beings have lived on plains as farmers and herders for thousands of years. Today, so many people live on the world's plains that their grasslands are threatened.

Farm Field
Tall Prairie Grass
Short Prairie Grass
Topsoil
Deep Roots

Where Are the World's Plains?

Like mountains and deserts, plains are one of Earth's most important landforms. These wide grasslands can be found throughout the world. Some are in hot areas near the **Equator**. The Equator is an imaginary circle around Earth, halfway between the North Pole and the South Pole. Some plains are in cold regions far to the north and south.

This map shows some of the world's largest plains. What are plains called in North America? What are the plains of central Africa called?

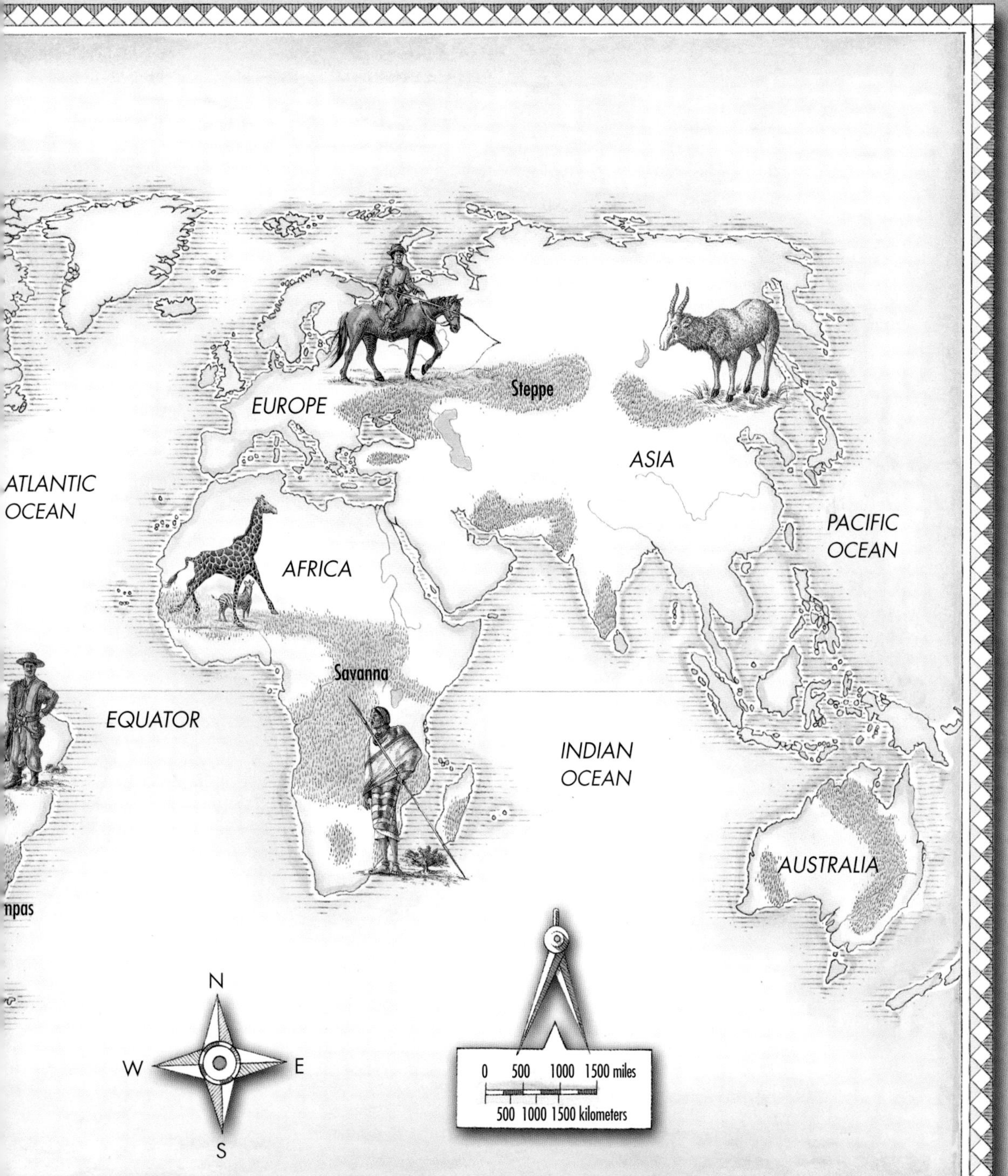
EUROPE
Steppe
ASIA
ATLANTIC OCEAN
PACIFIC OCEAN
AFRICA
Savanna
EQUATOR
INDIAN OCEAN
AUSTRALIA
npas
N
W
E
S
0 500 1000 1500 miles
500 1000 1500 kilometers

Rain, wind, and fire help grasses grow.

Storm clouds gathering over grasslands

Climate Makes Grasslands

Climate is the usual weather in a place. Plains are found in places where the climate is too dry for forests and too wet for deserts.

A prairie wildfire

Some plains receive most of their yearly rainfall in a very short time. Then many months can pass with little or no rain at all. Trees and bushes have a hard time surviving in such a dry climate, but grasses can. Their stems and leaves have a special way of storing water.

Wind and fire also help grasslands grow. Each year, the wind carries grass and wildflower seeds to new places. With each rain, new seedlings sprout, take root, and grow.

Summer storms bring lightning. When lightning strikes the ground, dry grasses can catch fire. Spread by the wind, wildfires burn the grasslands. The grasses grow back quickly, fed by the ashes in the soil. Soon, the burned ground is covered with new grass.

There are many words for "grassland."

A herder on the Mongolian steppes

Grasslands Have Different Names

A giraffe and wildebeests roaming the African savanna

Grasslands have different names in different parts of the world. **Savannas** are plains that stretch across the hot lands near the Equator. Savannas have widely scattered trees growing on them.

Farther away from the Equator, in areas with hot summers and cold winters, plains are often called **prairies**. Prairies that get very little rain have short grass. Prairies that get more rain can have grass 12 feet (3.6 meters) high. Prairies may have trees growing near water sources, such as springs or streams.

North American prairie

In very cold areas, plains are often called **steppes**. Steppes have very short grass and are largely treeless.

A woman from the steppes of central Asia

Plains provide food.

An American farm

People Farm on Plains

Plains are good places to farm. The soil of these grasslands is often deep and rich. Their flatness makes them easy to plow and harvest. Grains such as wheat and corn grow well on plains. These grains feed billions of people around the world. Cows, horses, and pigs also eat the grain and other crops grown on plains.

A farmer feeding his cows

The Great Plains region of the central United States has some of the richest farmland in the world. Farmers on the Great Plains know that grasses grow well there. They plant grass crops, such as wheat, oats, barley, alfalfa, and hay. These crops can survive in the dry climate of the Great Plains.

A farmer teaching her son about a wheat harvest

Plains grasses hold on to the soil.

Grass grows tall on plains.

Grasslands Protect Soil

Plains grasses have very long roots. Their roots can grow twice as deep underground as the grass grows above ground. These roots twist and tangle as they grow. They form a woven mat that holds down the topsoil.

On the Great Plains, clouds of dust blew over American farmland in the 1930s.

When people first began to farm the North American grasslands, they plowed up the land. They dug out the grasses and their long roots. They planted crops that did not have roots strong enough to hold the soil in place. During years of little rain, the soil dried out. When the winds came, the topsoil blew away in big dust clouds. With the rich topsoil gone, crops could not grow.

Farmers today have new ways to protect the soil. In some areas, people are planting the plains grasses again and turning farmland back into grassland.

Herding is a way of life on grasslands.

Masai herders watching their goats

Herders Live on Plains

Plains are good places for people who live by herding. It takes a lot of grass to feed **livestock**. This is what animals raised for meat, milk, and hides are called. Herders must keep moving so their animals don't graze in one place too long. The herders know new grass needs time to grow.

The Masai (mah–SI) people are herders on the plains of eastern Africa. For thousands of years, the Masai have raised cattle and goats on the savannas of Kenya and Tanzania. Their livestock provide meat and milk. The Masai use cowhide and goatskin to make clothes and bedding.

Herding is the Masai way of life. Masai herders never stay in one place for long. They move with their herds, crossing the savannas to find new grazing lands and fresh water.

A Masai boy begins to learn how to become a herder when he is five years old. He learns by watching over the calves. When he turns 15, a Masai boy is ready to take care of his own herd.

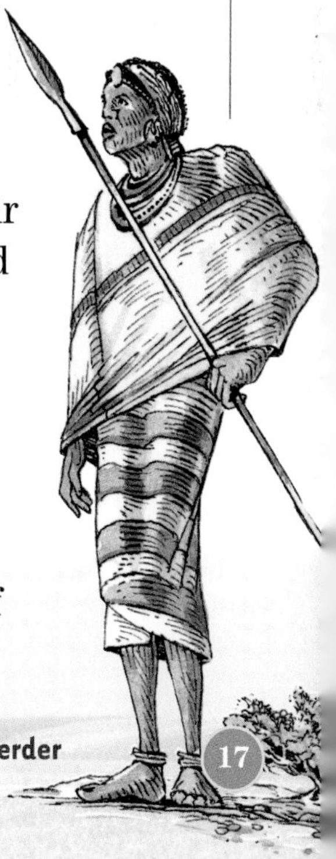

Masai herder

Ranching is big business on plains.

A gaucho using a lasso

Ranchers Need Grasslands

Plains with short rich grasses are good places for ranches. Wide plains provide ranchers with plenty of grazing land for their livestock. Unlike herders who move, such as the Masai, ranchers stay in one place. They build fences around big sections of the grasslands to keep their animals from wandering off.

In some parts of South America, a grassland is called a **pampa**. On the vast Pampas of Argentina, big ranches stretch for miles. The cowboys there, called gauchos, ride their horses across the Pampas. The gauchos round up cattle and mend broken fences. Each year, the gauchos drive their herds across the Pampas to corrals, or cattle pens, on the ranches. Then the cattle are taken to market and sold.

Ranchers in Argentina know they need to protect their grasslands. If their livestock overgraze the Pampas, the grass will not grow back. If big herds of cattle trample the ground too often, they destroy the stems and roots of the grass.

Plains have different kinds of wildlife.

Buffalo on the prairie

Plains Provide Habitats

Prairie dog

Hawk

Buffalo and calf

Plains are **habitats**, or natural homes, for many different kinds of plants and animals. No grassland is exactly like another. To start with, there are thousands of different kinds of grasses. Each plain's habitat has the grasses that are just right for that soil and climate.

Many kinds of animals find a perfect home on North America's prairies. Buffalo roam in protected grasslands. Golden eagles and hawks soar overhead, hoping to spot a mouse in the grass. Busy prairie dogs burrow into the prairie soil, building their underground towns. In the spring, people in Nebraska begin watching the sky for the return of thousands of sandhill cranes. Huge flocks of these big birds fly in to spend summer on the prairie by the Platte River.

Sandhill cranes

A cheetah on an African savanna

Plains Are Natural Wealth

Grasslands are a very important part of a country's natural wealth. They are valuable as farmland, as grazing land for livestock, and as a habitat for wildlife.

The Serengeti (ser–uhn–GET–ee) Plain is the most famous grassland in Africa. It covers thousands of square miles in eastern Africa. Many kinds of grasses grow there. They provide food and shelter for wildlife.

For thousands of years, herders such as the Masai were the only people who lived on the Serengeti Plain. Then farmers, ranchers, and big game hunters arrived. People worried that the savanna's habitat might be damaged. To protect it, they created Serengeti National Park.

Today, more than three million animals live in Serengeti National Park. People from all over the world travel there to look at wildlife. The visitors can see herds of wildebeests, gazelles, and zebra. Lions, cheetahs, and leopards hunt there, but people cannot.

A zebra

Plains inspire artists and writers.

A wheat field

Plains Are Beautiful

Plains have their own special beauty. In the early morning, dew sparkles on the grass. Big white clouds sail across the huge sky. The wind makes the plains ripple like a sea of grass. Birds dart from place to place, sending their songs into the air.

American artists, such as Thomas Hart Benton, have found beauty in the Great Plains. They paint its huge, simple landscapes of grass and sky.

Thomas Hart Benton, *Threshing Wheat*

The prairies have also inspired American writers. Laura Ingalls Wilder wrote about life on the Great Plains during pioneer days. In her famous book, *Little House on the Prairie*, Wilder described the wind blowing across the plains. She pictured the great sky curving over the endless grasslands. In *Sarah, Plain and Tall*, author Patricia McLachlan tells how a woman from the seashore came to love the Great Plains and its sea of grass.

Towns are covering grasslands.

This neighborhood is spreading over farmland.

Grasslands Are a Disappearing Resource

An earthmover and a bulldozer dig up prairie land.

Once, grasslands covered much of Earth. Today, millions of people live and work on the world's plains. As a result, their grasslands are threatened.

On huge farms, crops have taken the place of native grasses. Overgrazing by livestock has damaged the grasslands. People have dug up plains looking for such underground resources as coal and oil.

Cities and suburbs have spread. They cover grasslands with streets and houses, shopping centers, and parking lots. Land once carpeted in grass and wildflowers is now covered over by asphalt and concrete.

Human use of land changed plains habitats. Many plains animals and plants have lost their food supply and the protection of the grasses. Some animals, plants, and insects have disappeared from the plains.

Volunteers learning how to
plant seeds from their bags

People Bring Grasslands Back

Land in Illinois set aside for prairie conservation

In many parts of the world, people are working to protect and save the plains. They know that the loss of the plains' habitats and resources will affect everyone.

On the prairies of North America, people are learning from the mistakes of the past. Those who live and work there now practice **conservation**. This means that people are using natural resources wisely.

Grasses are the heart of the prairie. To bring them back, people raise money to purchase land from farmers and ranchers. They plant native grasses and wildflower seeds instead of food crops. National and state parks and nature preserves set aside land to protect the natural prairie habitat. By planting grasses and wildflower gardens, people in prairie states are helping to bring the grasslands back.

Visual Literacy

Photographs About Plains

Many nonfiction books include photographs. Photographs show how real people and places look. Photographs differ in the views they show of their subjects.

One important way in which photos differ is how close a view they give of their subject. A close-up photograph shows its subject from a very short distance. An aerial (AIR–ee–uhl) photograph shows its subject from far away. It is taken from a high place, such as a tall building, a mountaintop, or an airplane. It gives a bird's-eye view of its subject. Look at the photographs here as you follow these steps.

How to Read a Photograph

- **Read the caption or label.** This tells the subject of the photograph.
- **Look closely at the photograph.** Zoom in on details.
- **Think about what you see.** Ask yourself what the photograph tells you about its subject.

Thinking About the Photographs

- What does the close-up photograph show about a prairie fire? Write a short description of what it might be like to be near this fire.
- What additional information about prairie fires does the aerial photograph give you?

Close-up photograph of a prairie fire

Aerial photograph of a prairie fire

Glossary

climate the usual weather in a place

conservation the wise use of natural resources

Equator an imaginary circle around Earth, halfway between the North Pole and the South Pole

habitat the natural home of an animal or plant

livestock animals raised for meat, milk, hides, and other products

pampa a grassland in South America

plain a large area of flat land usually covered with grass

prairie a grassland in an area with hot summers and cold winters

savanna a grassland in a hot area near the Equator

steppe a grassland in a very cold area

topsoil the layer of soil on the surface of the ground